SANDBOX
WISDOM

Growing your business with the genius of childhood

Tom Asacker

To my father, for always
giving me the two things
I needed most —
trust and love.

And to my two Angels,
Alexandra and Andrea,
who will always have mine.

You have brains in your head,
and feet in your shoes.
You can steer yourself
in any direction
you choose.

~ Dr. Seuss

What's your brand? Is it your company? Your product? Your store? Your department? You? My dream — the dream that you have the power to make come true — is that this little book will help you separate the "truth" about branding, marketing, selling, and corporate culture from the "facts": all of those trendy and complicated techniques, theories, and concepts being promoted as magic potions for growth. And then, once you've rediscovered the "truth", you will go out, challenge the status quo, and really change things. You'll liberate your unique inner voice and inspire, innovate, and make profound improvements in yourself, your business, and in people's lives. You'll create a brand truly worthy of remark.

Sandbox Wisdom is a way for you to reconnect to those simple, yet powerful human "truths" that you once knew instinctively, but may have long since forgotten. It's a way to awaken the subconscious wisdom of your childhood and revitalize your business, and your life. Starting right now, stop waiting for others to lead and inspire you. Instead, do as Gandhi recommended and be the change that you want to see in others. After all, you do have brains in your head and feet in your shoes. You can steer yourself in any direction you choose.

CHAPTER *1*

Children guessed (but only a few) and down they forgot as up they grew...

~ e. e. cummings

Spreadsheets don't lie. The words repeated themselves in the CEO's head like a mantra. Spreadsheets don't lie.

"Bill? Bill?… You need anything? I'm leaving now."

The CEO looked up from his desk, a pile of spreadsheets and printouts covering every square inch of mahogany wood.

"Huh? No thanks. Go on home."

His assistant nodded. "You should too, you know. You look exhausted."

"I'll be heading out soon."

After his assistant shut the door, Bill again returned to his spreadsheets. He couldn't understand it. He had tried everything to push the company's performance back up to where it should be. He had hired consultants, sent key people to motivational conferences, invested heavily in technology and education, met with every department head as well as most of the employees. He had never spent so many exhausting hours at work. His wife said he'd become "a shadow husband."

I am in the shadows, he thought. Trying to make this company work again… and more in the dark than ever before.

The spreadsheets told of a corporation with sagging profits. Morale was at an all-time low; his own as well as his employees'. *Spreadsheets don't lie. What we're doing isn't working. So much for expensive consultants.*

Bill's phone rang. He looked at his Rolex. The irony wasn't lost on him. *I have all the trappings of success. Right down to my watch. But I can't make my company tick.* "Six-thirty? Where did the day go?"

He picked up the receiver.

"Bill West."

"Bill, it's Jim."

He instantly recognized the voice of his old college roommate. "Jim? How are you? I haven't spoken to you since... when? Last Christmas?"

"I'm doing great. I just got back from a vacation with Susan. Unbelievable trip. Before that, very busy. We're experiencing unprecedented growth. I am so pumped up about what's going on."

"That's great," Bill said, while his insides churned. The industry buzzed with talk of how his old friend had turned around sales in his division.

"How've you been, Bill?"

"The truth or the whitewashed version?"

"Between old friends? Truth, of course."

"Lousy. We're in a big-time slump. I'm in a big-time slump. I'm trying everything, but nothing's working."

"Well, I'm in town and I know it's kind of late notice, but do you want to meet for dinner?"

"Sure. Where are you staying?"

Within an hour, the two old friends were having a drink at a dark-wood-paneled steakhouse in the city.

"I don't want to monopolize the conversation, Jim. I do want to hear all about your trip and Susan and the kids. But I am just at my wit's end. What is going on here? Why aren't any of my methods working?"

"Maybe you're trying too hard."

"Nonsense, Jim. You and I have worked harder than anyone I know. But did it ever seem like work?"

"Not really."

"Yeah… sure there are times you feel frustrated, but it used to be enough to just get up in the morning. The passion. You still have that. And me? I can't see past the numbers. I can't see past the mess."

"Maybe you've hired too many consultants. Everyone has an opinion, but what's in your gut?"

"An ulcer."

The two men laughed as a waiter brought them thick slabs of prime rib.

"Listen," Jim said as he cut into his dinner, "can you stand one more opinion?"

"Sure."

"I think you need to see my guru."

"Guru? *You* went to see a guru?"

"Not a meditation guru, Bill. A business guru. At least that's what he is to me. And not just anyone. The best. Two years ago, I was where you are."

"I do remember now… sales were stagnant and profits were non-existent. But you totally turned that around."

"With a little help."

"Your guru?"

"Trust me, Bill?"

"Implicitly."

"Let me make a few phone calls tomorrow. I'm sure the guru will fit you in. Challenging cases intrigue him."

"I'll be ready. You just name the time and place."

That Thursday afternoon, Bill found himself driving to a gas station on the edge of town. Jim's instructions had been vague. Bill was supposed to be at the station by 1:15. He would leave his car there and the guru, a man named Richard Falcon, would meet him and drive them to their next destination.

"Everybody simply calls this guy Falcon. You know how some people fit their name?" Jim had said. "Well, this guy's got piercing vision."

Bill had stared at the directions as he took them down over the phone.

"Why can't I just meet him at our actual destination?"

"Listen Bill. It's how Falcon works. You gotta trust me."

"You're not sending me on some Outward Bound thing are you Jim? I'm not going to end up in some swamp with a compass and a Swiss Army knife and one day's supply of rations, am I?"

"Just trust me."

As Bill drove that Thursday to the appointed station, he mused; *I better not be going on some wild goose chase. I'm wearing my best Armani suit.*

He pulled his Lexus into the charming little service station. It had a quaint sign right out of the 1950s, and the adjoining mechanic's garage was painted crisp white. At the old-fashioned pump, stood the station's lone customer — a big man in an expensive suit leaning his elbow on a cherry-red Porsche. He was talking to a slim, silver-haired mechanic in blue overalls. At the sight of the man's tailored suit, Bill relaxed. *At least no wilderness adventure. This guy will know what I'm dealing with.*

He pulled into a parking spot, strode across the concrete to the big man, and extended his hand.

"It's a pleasure to meet you. I'm Bill West. Thank you so much for meeting me on such short notice."

The man raised his eyebrow and returned the firm handshake Bill proffered. "Nice to meet you, Bill. By any chance are you looking for Falcon?"

Bill nodded. "Well, then you need to meet this gentleman here," he gestured to the mechanic.

Bill tried to keep a startled expression off his face as he turned to the mechanic.

"Mr. Falcon, I'm Bill West. I'm sorry… I just assumed…"

"A pleasure to meet you," Falcon broke in, a bemused twinkle in his eye. "Come on, we have to hurry if we're going to make our next appointment."

Settled into a classic Barracuda, the two men headed down the highway.

"I brought all my spreadsheets, the performance charts from the last four quarters. Any fact or figure you need, I've got right here," Bill pointed at the briefcase he'd brought.

"Actually, we don't need them. We're on our way to meet our teacher."

"Great. Between the three of us, I sure hope we can get this company back on track. I wonder all the time . . . is it the marketing? The advertising? My sales team? What is it?"

"Trust me, this teacher will give you clarity that you've never had before. She helped me."

"She? Okay. Great. Was your garage not doing well?"

Falcon roared with laughter. When he finally stopped laughing, he smiled and spoke, "I used to head a multi-million dollar company that I built from the ground floor up. And that was in the pre-Internet days when profits mattered."

Bill stared at his new acquaintance, impressed.

"I wanted to take it public and then retire so I could pursue my hobby of restoring classic cars. The only problem was I felt completely stagnant. After a lifetime in business, I just couldn't get excited about it anymore. I lost my passion. And then I met our teacher. And everything changed forever."

The two men talked about companies and cars, and about fifteen minutes later, Falcon pulled the Barracuda up in front of an elementary school.

This guy has got to be kidding me. Our teacher is an actual teacher? Some kindergarten expert is going to teach me about marketing and profit margins? What was Jim thinking when he set this up? And now I'm stuck. I don't even have a car to make a graceful exit.

Falcon turned off the engine and looked at Bill with total compassion.

"Lesson number one, Bill. Keep an open mind. I know your brain is rattling through a thousand reasons why I'm a crackpot. I'm wearing overalls. My fingernails are dirty. And I've just taken you to a schoolyard. When you pulled into my station, did you guess I was a former CEO? Worth millions? I say that not to impress you, but to impress upon you that assumptions get you nowhere in life. They close doors, not open them. Come on… here's our teacher."

As Falcon said this, jubilant children streamed out of opened doors. A little girl ran towards Falcon, two long, black braids streaming behind her. She was missing her two front teeth-immediately evident in her grin. "Grandpa!" She threw her arms around Falcon's neck as he knelt to greet her. Cheeks flushed, she was the epitome of childish glee.

"Annie, I'd like you to meet Mr. West."

Bill knelt down and reached out a gentle hand, "It's very nice to meet you Annie."

"Nice to meet you too, Mr. West," Annie smiled, shaking his hand. "Do you have any kids?"

"No. Not yet. Maybe someday. I really like children."

"Good. Because I like most grown-ups. Not scary ones like the lunch lady who never smiles. But nice ones. And if you know Grandpa, you must be as nice as he is."

She removed her brightly-colored backpack and climbed into the back seat of the car, as Falcon opened the door. Bill looked at Falcon expectantly.

"Are we waiting for her teacher?"

"Her teacher? Oh… no. Annie *is* the teacher."

"What?"

"No assumptions, remember? And actually, she's not really our teacher. She's simply our assistant. Your experience with her is your teacher. See… only experiences have value. You experience something, you live through it, you know it."

"Yeah, but…"

"Listen, Bill. What holds people back from experiencing new things? Why do they limit their experiences? Because they perceive risks. Today, with me and Annie here, there are no risks. There are no customers, no shareholders, no media people — just you and me and one adorable little girl who's ready for her ice cream cone. What do you have to lose?"

"Nothing, I guess," Bill said as he slid into the front seat. *If nothing else, I can have a good laugh about this someday.* But he had to admit one thing, Falcon had an air of serenity and real happiness about him.

Hope it's contagious.

WISDOM,
begins in
WONDER.

~ Socrates

CHAPTER 2

We want people to feel with us more than to act for us.

~ *George Eliot*

Didn't you just pass a couple of Dairy Barns on this stretch of highway?" Bill asked Falcon as they continued driving.

"We never go there," Annie piped up from the back seat.

"Why not?"

"It's just not as good as Udder Delight."

"Never been there."

"It's delicious! And fun."

Well, I sure hope this ice cream is worth the drive, Bill thought to himself as they passed yet another sit-down ice cream parlor along the way. He looked in the back seat and noticed that Annie was engrossed in a book. He turned to Falcon.

"She's adorable."

"I think so, too. I also notice she seems to have no problem turning the pages. I want to thank you for that."

"What? Thank me for what?"

"Oh… just a joke. But I noticed when I introduced the two of you at the schoolyard that you knelt down and shook her hand very softly. You didn't give her one of those vise-like handshakes."

"Come on…like I'm going to crush your granddaughter's hand," Bill smiled.

"Of course not, I guess. Well, we're almost at Udder Delight. But I'll give you something to think about as you ponder what flavor you want."

"What's that?" Bill asked, eager to get on with the business aspect of their afternoon together.

"Why did you shake Annie's hand so gently?"

"Because she's a little girl."

"But I shook your hand at the station, and you had a strong grip."

"It wouldn't be appropriate to shake her hand like that."

"Ah-ha! You, my friend, have just had an Ah-ha moment. Do you realize it?"

"Sorry Falcon. Now I'm really lost."

"You said it wouldn't be *appropriate* to shake her hand with a vise grip. What I want to know is this: If, in business, you meet someone who has a gentle handshake, what do you do?"

"I give them my usual handshake. I was taught in business school — like everyone else for that matter — that the first greeting you offer in a business situation is a firm handshake. Leaves a strong impression."

"Uh-huh. Well, I think it's time to bury those B-school myths. That kind of handshake is all about showing off your power and strength. And Bill… people don't deal with you because they're impressed with you. They do it because they feel like it. Because they connect with you and trust you. And do you know who people trust — and bond with — the most?"

Bill looked down and to the left, obviously searching for the right answer.

"Think about children, Bill."

"Other children?"

"Exactly. They trust people like themselves. People with the same characteristics. So if someone has a soft handshake, give that person a soft one back. Acknowledge that you understand and respect that person. You want them to feel comfortable with you. Business is about connections, being comfortable and feeling safe with the person you choose to do business with. All this power stuff is old news. The way things used to be. Time for a change."

Bill nodded. "An Ah-ha moment."

"Precisely. A paradigm shift. A change in the way you think about the world. Because when you change your mind, Bill, *then* you change your life."

At that, Falcon pulled his Barracuda into the parking lot of a picturesque ice cream parlor that resembled a barn. As they entered, the owner, Mr. Garcia, greeted them with a wide smile. "Mr. Falcon. Welcome. Rum raisin today? Peppermint stick for the lady?"

"Rum raisin for me, Albert. But Annie might want to try something else. And Bill? Something for you?"

"I'll take a scoop of… hmm… I'll take a scoop of mint chocolate chip."

"Coming right up. I'll send it over to your usual booth. And in the meantime, I'll help Annie here to some first-class taste-testing."

Mr. Garcia turned all his attention to Annie. The parlor was fairly empty, with just two or three tables of people. Annie moved along the glass-enclosed freezer case, standing on tiptoe and peering in at the homemade ice cream. Like a child excited by the magic of a Christmas store display, she oohed and ahhed and took her time pointing out flavors and tasting each one very carefully.

Bill and Falcon sat at their booth and drank the ice water that had been brought out to them by a waiter in farmer's overalls.

"Cute place."

"Yeah. And wait'll you see how busy it gets when school lets out. You know, Bill, before all the commotion, I want to ask you another question. When you acknowledged my little Annie there at the schoolyard, you knelt down. You ever do that with a customer?"

"Get down on my knees? Sure, when I'm begging to close that big sale."

Falcon laughed, "No, I mean deal with them on their level."

"I don't know. I think I do."

"Really? On their level? Whatever that level is? Because when you say hello to someone, you're not just exchanging a bit of social pleasantry. You're doing a lot more. You're saying 'trust me.' Because, nowadays, people are extremely skeptical."

"Of course. I must deal with people on their level. I know that I can't stand it when someone gets past my assistant, and the call is just a cold call. Or being cornered by a phony at a meeting or a cocktail party."

"Sure. But go another level deeper. Why do you dislike it so intensely?"

"I don't know. I guess I feel… used. Like this person could care less about my time and doesn't really want to talk to me. They want to talk to my wallet."

"Exactly, Bill. Many people have forgotten—in this technological age—

Many people have forgotten how to **slow down***, truly empathize and make each contact count as a* **genuine***, sincere encounter. It's still all* **about people** *and their* **feelings.**

how to slow down, truly empathize and make each contact count as a genuine, sincere encounter. It's still all about people and their feelings. But we all seem to have forgotten that."

Falcon sighed and looked off into the distance. Then he refocused on Bill, who had taken out a small leather notebook and a Mont Blanc pen.

"I hear you, Falcon. I've forgotten some of this myself. I want to write all this down so I don't forget it again."

"Okay, but remember, today is about our experience. So it's more important that you take notice than to take notes. Got it?"

"I understand. And I hear you about customers' feelings. I know I get busy and forget that. I just don't have the time the way I used to."

"Can't let that happen. You're in the feelings business, Bill. Everyone is. You need to focus on the experience your customers and your employees have with you and your company. Respect, authenticity, empathy, being vulnerable."

"Grandpa!" Annie came running over with her ice cream cone. "Peppermint stick is still my favorite."

"Well… there's always next time. Tastes change. But until then, you're still my peppermint stick sweetie." Annie smiled.

"Here." Falcon fished into his pocket. "Why don't you go play the jukebox." He counted out eight quarters. "This is enough for six songs. Though, Annie, when I was a kid a handful of nickels kept the jukebox going all night long."

Annie departed the table again, clutching her cone and her quarters.

"You are unbelievably good with her," Bill West's voice was admiring.

"Naw. Just real. You see, Bill, that's why I said you'd learn a lot from spending the afternoon with Annie as your teacher. If you think like a child, if you become the child, you can learn all the secrets to revitalizing your business sense. Did you watch the owner with Annie? He offered her no less than nine tastes of ice cream. And he never hurried her, even though he knew as well as I that she would choose the peppermint stick in the end. You see… kids don't like to be rushed. No one does. And Albert understands that. But what's happened with the advent of technology? We try to make trust grow in a nanosecond. We don't develop it." Falcon paused and glanced at the door. "Say Bill… what time is it?"

"Three o'clock."

"Oh boy! Watch out. The masses arrive soon. School's out at the high school and junior high."

"Should we leave?"

"No. Let's just observe."

Annie rejoined them and quietly sat eating her ice cream cone and listening to the music of her juke box selections as students streamed in.

"This is worse than a 70s disco," Bill remarked. "They're three deep at the counter."

Yet they watched as Albert Garcia and his employees masterfully handled the crowd of students. Amazingly, the proprietor seemed to know most of the students by name, and he doled out praise and encouragement with each scoop.

"Joey, how did that history test go?"

"Great Mr. G. I aced it."

"Second scoop's on me!"

Then he turned to his next customer. "You cut your hair, Amy. I like it. Are you happy with it?"

A shy girl nodded.

"Good. I think the haircut suits you."

Falcon turned to Bill West at the table, "Did you see how that girl's face just lit up when he noticed her hair?"

"Yeah. She's a pretty girl."

"Sure. But she's an adolescent. She doesn't always feel that. But he made her feel good. He noticed it. Do you do that with your customers and your people? Notice something that is meaningful to them?"

"No. Seems kind of fake to offer compliments like that."

"Fake? More B-school myth. Our needs, as adults, are not much different from childhood

Your job is **people** *and their* **feelings.**

needs. We need to feel complimented, praised, valued. If you look for opportunities to praise others it will change your whole outlook on life. I guarantee it."

"It will, huh?" Bill raised a skeptical eyebrow as he polished off the last of his ice cream.

"Sure. Instead of looking for the negative, you'll spend your time looking for the positive. Your outlook will change. What is that indefinable something that makes us want to be with someone?"

"Energy?"

"Energy and the fact that they're giving us their pure feelings. And if you look for a compliment, if you look for praise, if you look for ways to reward someone's accomplishments—an employee's, a customer's, a supplier's —with genuine words of thanks and real appreciation and admiration on your part, the positive energy you receive back will be a hundredfold."

"But I get so caught up in things at work. Am I going to remember to stop and notice these things about my customers and my employees?"

"If you don't, I can assure you things won't turn around. These things you get caught up in at work—your in-box and to-do list—are not your job. Your job is people and their feelings. Being focused on others is the key to finding true success. Look at the crowd here. You think the other ice cream places are like this? Albert and his employees never get frustrated. And they attend to all of the little details."

"I can see why the place is popular. And my ice cream was *udderly delightful.*"

"I'm telling you . . . the rum raisin is the best. Now, Annie Bananie, where to next?"

"The park. Did you bring the bread?"

"Have two loaves of day-old under the front seat."

Bill looked quizzically at Falcon.

"We're duck people," Annie explained. "We like to feed them at the pond near the park."

"Well, let's go then. And ice cream's on me. This was worth ten thousand ice creams," Bill said as he went to pay, suddenly sure he would learn more lessons at the duck pond.

Bill's Notepad

* People respond to genuineness. Make sure we don't lose sight of this.

* We respond to others who are like us. Next company meeting, tell the story about the hand-shake-thing that Falcon told me. They'll all relate, I think.

* It's about feelings. We're in the feelings business. Get everyone in the company to say this over and over 'til they mean it.

* Be empathetic and provide a memorable experience, not just good customer service.

CHAPTER 3

You can observe a lot by watching.

- Yogi Berra

"If you had told me a week ago that I would find a trip to an ice cream store 'enlightening,' I would have called you crazy."

"Visionaries risk being misunderstood, Bill. What we must remember is we are trying to change the world."

"The world? I'd settle for a solid quarter of profits and happy stockholders."

"The world is not a static thing. We're part of it. We can change it. You simply have to be willing to risk being vulnerable and open."

Bill glanced in the back seat at Annie, contentedly looking out her window, as crowded suburbs became more pastoral.

"It's easy to be vulnerable with sweet kids like Annie. But what about the sharks in the corporate waters?"

"Bill, history has shown us that what makes heroes interesting is not simply their great strengths but also their weaknesses. I've learned more from my granddaughter than from all the great books I've read or courses I've taken. The wisdom of children is their inability to conceal their feelings. Honesty and vulnerability isn't perceived as weakness. It's what makes them unique and endearing to us."

Falcon made a left-hand turn into a beautiful park and drove toward the duck pond. Couples strolled arm in arm, a few teens whizzed by on in-line skates, and children ran under the watchful gazes of their mothers.

"Mr. West," Annie called out from the back seat. "Did you know that if you smile at people they smile back?"

Bill turned his head to look at Annie. "That's because they love that grin of yours. Did the tooth fairy visit?"

She nodded. "I got a dollar. A silver dollar!"

Falcon winked at Bill. "A value-added dollar. Same purchasing power, but a whole lot prettier to hold."

Annie waved out the window. "Sometimes people even wave back. I sometimes have a contest with my cousin, Frank. We each wave at people out different windows and see who gets the most waves back."

"When our culture stopped waving and saying hello," Falcon said softly, "we lost our connection to others."

"Agreed. And the headphones sure haven't helped."

Falcon pulled into a parking lot, and they all climbed out of the car and began walking in the general direction of the duck pond. Annie skipped and whistled and waved at passersby.

Bill turned to Falcon. "I've been thinking about our lessons at Udder Delight."

"And?"

"One thing kind of bothers me. What if I don't *feel* like smiling, or waving, or complimenting someone? If I do it anyway, it seems fake. Almost like acting. And the handshake thing… if I change my style to match someone else's, I'm not being authentic."

"But we all take on roles when we're dealing with others,

PEOPLE RESPOND TO *smiles.*

Bill. Just because you try on that role doesn't mean that part of you, that role, isn't a 'real' part of you, an authentic part of you. When was the last time you went out for dinner?"

"Last week I took my wife out for dinner. To Antonio's over on 15th Avenue to just talk. Have an evening of conversation."

"Did you like that place? Would you recommend it to a friend?"

"Sure. Antonio's is a little expensive, but the food is great. The service was excellent. Four stars in my book."

"You say the service was excellent. Did you have a waiter or a waitress?"

"Waitress. She was good. Not too obtrusive, but just the right amount of friendliness."

"Do you think she loved being on her feet all night? You think she enjoyed rushing over to the inevitable crabby diner who wanted to send back his

29

food? Racing back and forth to the hot kitchen?"

"Loved it? No." Bill replied. "But it's not her job to love it. She's *supposed* to be friendly. Service with a smile, right?"

"Precisely. It's her *job* to be friendly and smile. To make you feel comfortable, to serve your wife and you in a courteous, professional manner. But she put *your* emotional needs ahead of her own. I see that as an act of caring. It doesn't matter if it's her job. You didn't know if she was tired or if she just had a fight with her husband or roommate before she came to work. She slipped into her *role* of professional server. It's all about heart. It's asking 'How do I dress to make the other person comfortable? How do I speak? How do I shake hands?' That attention to empathy conveys strength and caring and composure. These qualities attract us and reassure us." Falcon smiled as he watched Annie head toward a flock of geese and ducks. "Just as they did when we were small and helpless."

"Grandpa! Grandpa! Charlie's back!"

"Charlie?" Bill looked around and saw no one else was at the duck pond.

"He's that big white duck there with the soiled feathers. We used to see him all the time. Then he left the pond last winter, and he hasn't been back since. He's Annie's favorite."

Annie took one of the bags of bread from Falcon and approached the flock. Ducks and geese eagerly honked and quacked and grabbed at the bread. Some caught pieces mid-air, a feat that delighted Annie.

"They do tricks!" she squealed.

PEOPLE ARE LIKE DUCKS.

One bad experience can make them back away from us.

Other ducks and geese stayed back, satisfied to nibble at the crumbs and cast-offs of the more forward flock members. Charlie was one of them.

"Charlie? What's wrong, Charlie?" Annie approached the duck several times, trying to offer him large hunks of bread, but he backed away nervously.

"Grandpa? What's wrong with Charlie? Last year he was my friend."

"I don't know, Honey. Try standing still. Maybe he just doesn't remember you."

Falcon and Bill moved in closer for a look at the duck.

"He's definitely spooked," Bill said. "And his left wing doesn't rest right across his back."

Falcon motioned Bill back to a large oak tree. Then he whispered, "You know, there was this kid here last year, and I used to catch him throwing rocks at Charlie here. Who knows? Maybe Charlie was wounded one time."

"That's a shame."

"Well… ducks aren't all that different from people."

"This I have to write down," Bill laughed, taking out his pen and paper. "You, Falcon, can find meaning in just about anything. So tell me: How are ducks like people?"

"Well, you've already learned that birds of a feather flock together," Falcon joked. "Let me give you another insight. If they have good experiences, they return to you. If they have bad experiences, they won't be back. One time in which they are not shown empathy is enough to ruin their relationship with people. In ducks, it may be a rock. In humans, it may be a situation where their emotional needs were not recognized. Or worse… were ignored."

"I hear you."

"Grandpa! Oh my gosh come here! Come here!!!!" Annie was jumping up and down frantically pointing with excitement at the pond's edge. Falcon and Bill raced to her side.

"You see her? See? There… you shoulda seen the… there!!!!"

"What honey? Where?"

"There! There!" Annie was pointing so haphazardly that the two men didn't see she was drawing their attention to a small group of baby ducklings hiding in the reeds. Finally, Bill spotted the babies.

"Look, Falcon. There at the water's edge. To the left of that log."

"Shhh!" Falcon urged. The three fell silent and watched as the mother came to tend to her ducklings. After a few moments, Falcon whispered, "Let's give them a little privacy." They moved away and Falcon gave Annie another bag of bread, as he and Bill retreated to their position under the oak tree.

"She was so excited, at first I didn't know what she was pointing at."

"That's my granddaughter. No inhibitions. She's so alive. And you know, when you speak to people, you want them to leave with that same kind of enthusiasm. Just energy, pure and simple. People are persuaded by those who show passionate interest."

After Annie had finished with the second bag of bread, she joined the two men. Looking up in their oak tree, she exclaimed, "Grandpa, there's

Look at other perspectives. Always ask myself:

WHAT COLOR IS THEIR BIRD?

a bluebird up there."

"A blue jay?" Bill asked.

"No. Some other kind of blue bird. I know blue jays. They're mean to the other birds."

Bill and Falcon looked up. Bill squinted, "He's a green bird, Annie. Though I'm not sure what kind of bird either."

"Blue. I can see him perfectly."

Bill insisted, "He's a real deep green. Maybe someone's parakeet got loose."

"Blue." Annie giggled, but she was equally insistent and crossed her arms.

"Green," Bill joked in return.

Falcon said nothing, just walked around the tree several times. Finally, he spoke, "Whoever is wrong buys sodas at the snack stand."

"Deal," Annie said confidently.

"Bill, come over here." Bill proceeded over to Falcon, who was now kneeling on the ground. "Lie down right here, where Annie was standing a second ago."

"Lie down? With this suit on?"

"Yup."

Bill felt foolish, but he sat down on the grass and then leaned back to a reclining position. "From this vantage point, the bird is blue. I don't believe it."

"Some birds' feathers hit the light different. The sheen changes things. Guess sodas are in order," Falcon laughed heartily as he helped Bill up from the ground.

"Sorry, Annie. I was certain he was green."

Annie took his hand. "That's OK. I knew he was blue all along."

They walked together, Falcon at Bill's side.

"You know what that was called?" Falcon whispered.

"A blue bird?"

"Participant observation."

"Interpret that for me?"

"It's what ethnographers and cultural anthropologists do. Walk in another's shoes. In business, you can ask others questions, but you're just going to get an answer from their present perspective. What they think at the time. And sometimes they can't even describe it to you. So you have to do what they do. Lie down on the ground and see: What color is their bird?"

"I like that. A well-earned soda. Now where to?"

"Sodas. Then the sandbox. You ain't seen nothin' yet."

Bill grinned, Annie's hand tucked in his own. "Falcon, I'm pretty sure you're right!"

Bill's Notepad

* Children respond when you are genuine and vulnerable to them. So do adults. Let's cut out the pretentious nonsense and get real in everything we do from advertising, selling... to managing, etc.

* Everyone must adopt the appropriate caring role when they're with others. This doesn't make that role false. It's simply another side of ourselves.

* The wisdom of children is in their inability to disguise their feelings. I must be more childlike.

* Heroes are admired because of their strengths— and their weaknesses.

* Excitement is a palpable energy that is contagious. We must always leave our customers with that feeling.

* I must get out of my office and actually experience my employees and my customers' perspectives. Always ask myself about others: WHAT COLOR IS THEIR BIRD?

CHAPTER 4

The heart has its reasons that the mind cannot comprehend.

~ Blaise Pascal

At the snack stand, Bill treated Annie to a snow cone, Falcon to a soda, and he got himself a soda and a hot dog smothered in mustard.

"I have to say, this afternoon out of the office has turned out so downright pleasurable I feel guilty," he chuckled half to himself as he savored his junk food. "I never eat hot dogs anymore."

They found a shady picnic table under a tree and watched a nearby boy fly an elaborate trick kite.

"Can I go closer to watch him, Grandpa?"

"Sure Sweetie. Just don't wander off. Stay right there where I can see you."

Annie took her snow cone and approached the boy, who appeared several years older than Annie. He happily showed off for her, making the kite dip and turn.

"You know, Bill," Falcon said, "I've been thinking about our poor duck."

"Yeah . . . me too. Seems such a shame that someone would hurt him."

"Yeah. Trust is a tenuous thing. And you know, I thought of something else about him."

"What's that?"

"Over the winter, we didn't see Charlie. And then this spring, Annie and I have done other things—museum trips, visits to the library—so the duck had no contact with us for a long time. Even if Charlie wasn't abused, he would have been skittish. Ducks need frequency of contact. Just like people."

"You're probably right."

"Think about it. Have you ever had a friend you hadn't seen in a long, long time? And then you see that your school is having a reunion, or you run into your friend's mother and she urges you to call him. What do you do?"

"Honestly? I'm really uptight. I think 'What if this guy doesn't want to hear from me. We lost touch . . .'"

"Exactly. Me too. And customers are the same. If they don't see us over and over again, they assume the worst. 'I've been forgotten; that company didn't really care about my business; they're just like all the others.' Psychologists say that we have a natural tendency to like that which is familiar to us—that which we deal with over and over and over again. And those things or people we *don't* see…"

"I get it. So the lesson is feed the ducks often," Bill joked.

"Something like that. Don't *assume* you are making frequent contact.

TRUST, *EMPATHY*

Guarantee that you are. Let your company be depended on—known for—that kind of connection."

"You know, Falcon, I've been thinking about Annie's blue bird. When I kept trying to insist her bird was a different color, I never succeeded in changing her mind."

"Of course not. It's a waste of time—and in business, a big waste of money—to try to do that with people. We all have too much of ourselves invested in our worldview. Our beliefs, our values, even our prejudices have been established through a lifetime of choices. We can try to be open-minded, but face it, we all make assumptions."

"Like when I assumed my contact would be driving a Porsche, not wearing overalls. What an idiot…"

"Not an idiot, just human. We all assume. So the only way we can understand our customers' expectations, anticipate those expectations,

and *integrity* CAN'T BE COPIED.

make a connection, is by entering into and respecting their way of seeing the world. Children teach us this. That we must acknowledge their feelings—their worldview—before trying to help. Why do we forget and not apply this to adults?"

Bill finished the last bite of his hot dog and shook his head. "You know, Falcon, I really feel like I've learned a great deal today. I've enjoyed today—enjoyed your granddaughter immensely—but I just think this is all too simple. Anyone can understand this. I need advice that will help me run a hundred-million-dollar corporation . . . that can take me into the future."

Falcon looked disappointed. "So Bill… if it's so simple, why isn't everyone doing it? I'll tell you why. Most smart men and women—people like you with your advanced degrees and years of business experience—have lost faith in simplicity. You believe that for something to be valuable, it has to be complex. What's most valuable is that which can not be copied. And what can't be copied in this technological age is mastering the complex human relationships that remain the bedrock of any business. Trust, empathy and integrity, Bill, cannot be copied."

Annie was by this time holding on to the kite string herself. She was, from their vantage point, having a ball. Soon, however, the wind died and the kite came crashing down. The boy appeared to say something to Annie, and she came running over.

"I don't understand," her lip quivered. "He said he's not going to fly anymore today. The wind went away. But why can't he just run real fast and get the kite up again?"

"Maybe he could, Annie," Bill said, swinging his legs over the seat of the picnic table and squatting next to her. "But then what do you think would happen to the kite when he stopped running?"

"It would fall back down?"

"That's exactly right, Annie! To hold the kite up in the air, the wind has to catch it and float it up there," Bill said gently. "Usually about this time of the day, the wind dies down. That's probably it for kite flying today."

Crestfallen, Annie slumped on the picnic bench.

"Weren't we headed for the sandbox anyway?" Bill asked her. "It doesn't matter if the air is still over there."

Annie looked up, a hint of promise in her eyes. "Well? Are we going? Are we?"

The two men smiled and stood.

"To the sandbox!" Bill West joked and raised his arm like a Cavalry officer.

"Let's go!" Annie dashed off ahead of them, leading the way.

"Bill . . . I noticed in your kite explanation that you resisted flat out telling Annie the answer."

"And your point is?"

"I'm just guessing here, Bill, but I bet sometimes you can't resist letting your customers know that you're the expert and that you've figured out the solution to their problem. You just have to let them know."

"Well…"

"Listen Bill. It's perfectly fine to be smarter than others, if you can. Just make sure to be wise, and never let them know it. Help them discover the answer on their own, like you did with Annie. Everyone needs to feel smart and empowered. Not just kids."

Bill gazed at the horizon and nodded, as he quietly contemplated his most recent sales presentation.

At the sandbox, Annie approached two children playing with some buckets and shovels, and in no time, the three were playing together happily.

"There's my usual bench," Falcon motioned, and the two men sat and quietly watched the children.

Bill took out his pen and notebook, "Let me take a few minutes to scribble a note or two. I'm telling you, I haven't felt this energized in a while."

Falcon smiled. "Good. Me? I'm going to watch these kids at play. Look at Annie. She hasn't looked over at us once," Falcon spoke quietly. "Look at how they're all getting along. Me? I'm out of sight, out of mind."

"Does that hurt your feelings a little?"

"No. It's as it should be. And you know, our customers do that, too. We humans are a pretty predictable bunch."

"What are they doing now?"

The other little girl and boy and Annie were lying down in the sand and moving their arms and legs. Then the three of them stood up.

Someone once said,

"The **SECRET**

of genius is to carry

the **SPIRIT** of the

child into old age."

"Sand angels!" They screamed in unison.

Bill and Falcon shared a hearty laugh.

"Now I've seen everything," Bill chuckled.

"Well, they certainly are creative. Then again, they don't have the same inhibitions as we do. They're not afraid of getting dirty or looking a little foolish."

"They're covered in sand! Look at Annie's hair!"

"Cute, huh? My car is going to be full of sand tonight. You see, Bill, we think that kind of creativity and imagination is great when you're seven. But when you get into corporate culture, everyone's afraid to play. Afraid to look foolish or make a mistake. We have a tendency to be so serious. We look down on spontaneity and child-like ingenuity."

Lead them to the *solution.*

"I guess that goes along with what you were saying about people at the top, thinking solutions can't be simple."

"Precisely. But that's all wrong. I recall a great thinker who once said, 'Genius is childhood recaptured at will.'"

"Well, those three are certainly little geniuses. Making 'snow' angels in the sand."

The two men sat in silence, watching the three children playing. Suddenly, an argument appeared to break out over one of the sand tools they were using to construct an elaborate castle.

"Should we go help them sort it out?" Bill asked.

"No. I try to let Annie learn how to manage her own feelings."

Annie abruptly stood up, folded her arms across her chest and stomped her way over to Falcon. She was angry, but both Falcon and Bill could hear the frustration in her voice.

"I had it first and Mike said I could use it, and then Jessica took it away from me and it's not even hers!"

Falcon soothed his granddaughter with gentle words about the difficulties of sharing and the importance of compromise.

"Couldn't you offer to let Jessica use it for five minutes and then you could use it?" Bill asked. "I could let you know when five minutes is up. I could set my watch alarm."

"I guess I could," Annie shrugged. She wiped her face with the back of her hand and went back over to her playmates. Soon, peace seemed to reign in the sandbox again.

"See how you didn't vilify the other children, Bill?"

"Hmm?" Bill was setting his watch alarm.

"You didn't tell Annie, 'Gosh, that other little girl is so mean or selfish.'"

"Well, no, it's just kid stuff."

"Kid stuff, huh? Unique to kids, right?"

"Exactly."

"So, with children, we should hear anger as pain or as frustration. We shouldn't hear it as anger. We also shouldn't let it draw us in. But with adults, it's different?"

"I never really thought about it that way."

"Bill. How often do you do that in business? Get drawn into the middle of something that really is best resolved with a healthy dose of empathy?"

"I have a tendency to get in the cross fire between my people. And you're right. I hear how angry they are. I hear rage, sometimes—desk-pounding screaming fits. But what I don't hear are those sandbox clues."

"Sandbox clues," Falcon grinned. "Now you're the one coming up with this stuff. What are sandbox clues?"

"Well, in some ways, my people are acting like kids in a sandbox. At times, they have a desperate need to be heard or understood, just like Annie did. But I don't hear that. I hear it as a full-scale war, and I have to

*"Well, in some ways, my people are acting like **KIDS** in a sandbox.*

*At times, they have a **DESPERATE** need to be **HEARD** or **UNDERSTOOD,***

just like Annie did."

get involved. You know Falcon, I suppose the same thing can happen with angry customers or suppliers."

"And?"

"And... I have to make sure that my people slow down. Tune the world out—including their own emotional reactions—and tune our customers in. We must genuinely care about the pain or fear or whatever emotion is behind that anger. Again, those sandbox clues."

"I like that insight Bill."

Bill's alarm went off and he shouted over to the sandbox.

"Time to switch."

Peace continued in the sandbox.

"I wish all my people's conflicts were so simple to resolve."

"They can be. If we contain it in the sandbox and don't let it spill over."

"I hear you."

The two men continued watching the children, but Bill West's mind was churning in circles. Could it all be this simple? Had he simply forgotten those qualities of genuineness, empathy, vulnerability, and creativity? Could he do as Falcon urged? Could he recapture his childhood at will?

Bill's Notepad

* Frequency ensures comfort. Make sure our people are maintaining contact with our customers. Feed the ducks often—our new mantra.

* Be smarter than our customers— but help them arrive at solutions. Don't try to point out just how smart we are.

* Empathy and integrity can't be copied. That has to be our competitive edge.

* Encourage child-like ingenuity and creativity in the workplace.

* It's easier to empathize with children, but we must make our empathy with adults run just as deeply and sincerely. It's more important to be kind, than it is to be right!

* Watch for sandbox clues during all communications, especially conflicts.

CHAPTER 5

The truth is more important than the facts.

~ Frank Lloyd Wright

Bill West found himself staring at the clouds floating above the playground. He knew, on any other day, despite his corner office with its magnificent view of the city, he wouldn't have noticed the skyline, let alone the sky. He would have been concentrating on his spreadsheets; answering phone calls in rapid-fire succession. He would never have seen the perfect white clouds overhead.

The sky, he decided, looked surreal; dreamlike. The blue was too clear, too crisp, too perfectly… blue. Not even a master like Michelangelo, not even the Sistine Chapel he had marveled at two years ago on a trip to Italy, could duplicate the perfection of nature's masterpiece. Each cloud was so fluffy it looked as if it was made of the softest spun cotton. The air was so clean and crisp, and there were no sounds of phone lines jangling, people talking, footsteps pounding across office floors as employees raced to and fro. No, the sounds were of children laughing and the wind rustling leaves. He shut his eyes for a moment and was transported back to his own childhood. Suddenly, he felt profoundly reminiscent. Falcon jolted him from his mood, but it was as if he was reading Bill's mind.

"What would you have been if you hadn't gone into business?" Falcon directed his question to Bill as both their gazes ventured to the children playing in the sandbox.

Bill took a moment to collect his thoughts. "Honestly? If I wasn't so driven, I probably would have done something to help animals. Would have been a vet, but I was lousy in biology."

"You have any pets?"

"A few. We've got two dogs—an Akita, and a loveable mutt who wandered into our lives six years ago and never left. My wife has had her cat for fourteen years—an old, fat tabby named Mac. And we have a couple of canaries."

"A regular menagerie."

"Yeah. You could say that. It's a side of me people don't ordinarily see. But with what you've said about making yourself vulnerable… perhaps it's a side people should see."

"I think so. It's like Annie here. Even before I sold the company, when she was just a baby, I used to bring her into the office from time to time, show her off. Can you tell I'm the proudest grandfather on the planet? The days she came in reminded all of us in the company that we're human. Even the CEO gets down on his hands and knees and crawls around with the baby. And there's nothing wrong with that. We should be vulnerable. We don't have to be gods to our employees."

"What about you, Falcon? What would you have done if you hadn't been a captain of industry?"

"Me? I would have been a magician."

"A magician?"

"Yup. Then I could've spent all of my time playing with children—small ones like Annie there, and big kids, like me!"

With that, Falcon bounded off the bench and sprang onto his hands.

"Ha!" he shouted, "I can still do a handstand!" He held his pose for another moment before righting himself again.

"You know any magic tricks?"

"Do I know any magic tricks? Watch, my friend. And remember two words: truth and fact."

"Truth and fact? They're the same thing, aren't they?"

"Far from it, Bill. Far from it."

With that, Falcon strode over to the children. He sat on the wooden edge of the sandbox, with his feet in the sand and gathered Mike, Jessica, and Annie around his knees.

His first trick was every grandfather's favorite. He pulled a silver dollar from his pocket and made it disappear. Then he pulled it out of Mike's ear, much to the children's delight.

"Do it again! Do it again!" They screamed in unison.

Falcon happily obliged, pulling a silver dollar out of Jessica's ear, then Annie's. The children poked and probed in both ears, as if more coins were hidden there.

"You know," Falcon said, "I suppose you each need a silver dollar." With that he took a white handkerchief out of his other pocket. Then he squeezed and tugged at his nose with elaborate and loud sound effects that drove the children into fits of laughter. Suddenly, with a shocked expression on his face, three coins appeared in his handkerchief. "These must belong to each of you," he said as he handed the large, shiny coins to his audience.

"OK kids, now for this trick I need an assistant. Or maybe three assistants." He picked up a handful of sand and slowly poured it into his clenched fist. He held his fist out in front of each of the children and one by one he had them blow on his hand. Then the children shouted out some magic words, and with a flourish, Falcon opened his hand.

"The sand disappeared!" Mike grabbed Falcon's hand and stared at it. "How'd you do that?"

"A good magician never reveals his secrets." Falcon stood and bowed to his audience. Annie and her friends cheered loudly.

When Falcon rejoined Bill on the bench, Bill clapped. "Bravo! Not bad for an amateur magician, there, Falcon. I know the old coin-in-the-ear trick, but I have to admit I'm not sure how you did the sand trick."

"It's all about perception."

"I sense I'm about to learn something profound here," Bill ribbed his new friend.

"Actually Bill, it's not deep at all. I simply want to remind you that there is often a big difference between the facts—what you know and believe about your company or products—and your audience's truth, or their perception."

"Like your magic trick."

"Precisely. You see, the *truth* is that the kids all saw the sand go into my

Subjective reality

has its own set of rules.

Customers' reality

—*THEIR TRUTH*—

is what's important.

WE CAN'T FORGET THAT.

fist. The truth is what's believed. The *fact* was that the sand never really did go into my hand. But what those kids believe—their truth—is far more important than facts. Their perception is that I can make sand disappear. They believe it. That makes it so."

"I believed it." Bill smiled.

"Do you like magic?"

"Yeah. I actually do."

"Hold out your hand."

Falcon grabbed Bill's wrist, turned his palm face up and poured sand from his seemingly empty fist onto Bill's hand.

"OK, now I am thoroughly in awe. This sand seems awfully real to me."

"Listen, Bill. You and I both know magic always boils down to some kind of trick. And while we might have fun trying to figure out how the magician made the elephant disappear—or made the sand appear out of thin air— we love it when we can't figure it out. When we can believe in the magic and be transported for a few minutes or an hour or whatever. And the best marketing or sales is like the best performance. Your audience gets lost in it. They feel the benefit, rather than it being overt or obvious."

"Sure. You don't want your marketing to be dull."

"But it's much more than that, Bill. How about the story of the two competing neighborhood candy stores. Everything was pretty much the same at both establishments—same selection, same prices, same quality— but the neighborhood kids preferred one store over the other."

"The difference was the service, huh?" Bill interjected.

Falcon smiled. "Well… to an extent. But not the way you're probably thinking. Both owners were extremely friendly, and responsive. The problem was one of *truth* versus *fact*. You see, when the kids were asked why they preferred one store over the other they replied, 'Because the lady in the 'good' store always gives us extra candy. The lady in the 'bad' store always takes candy away.'"

Bill looked at Falcon with a puzzled expression. "Wait a minute, Falcon. I thought you said everything was the same at both stores. You didn't say that one store gave out extra candy with each order."

Falcon laughed. "The *fact,* Bill, is that the lady in the 'good' store *didn't* give extra candy. She simply put a small amount of candy on the scale and slowly kept adding to it. On the other hand, the lady in the 'bad' store would pile a heaping load of candy on the scale and then take candy away until she reached the correct weight. The facts—same amount of candy—didn't matter to the kids. Only *their* truth mattered. So, Bill, the lesson is…"

"I must make sure to always *add* to my customers' experience?"

Falcon smiled. "That too. But this particular lesson is that the key to successful marketing is to discover your customers' *truths*. What they feel is true. If you discover, uncover, and satisfy their unique emotional needs, you will, in their subjective reality, be the company, the salesperson, the supplier they want to do business with."

"This I'm jotting down," Bill said, pulling out his trusty pen.

FORGET *the* GOLDEN *Rule!*

Falcon paused. "You ready for a little shocker?"

"Sure," Bill said, pen poised.

"You know the golden rule? Do unto others…"

"…as you would have them do unto you. Absolutely. Who could forget it?"

"I want you to, Bill. I want you to never, ever follow the golden rule in a business setting with your customers."

"What?!"

"I'm serious. What makes you think that what you want or how you want to be treated is the same for them? Instead, you must do unto your customers as they *uniquely* want done unto them. Give them exactly what they want, when, where, and how they want it. Serve them the way *they* want to be served. The intangible benefits of emotions and feelings will be realized."

"I got you."

"And when we talked about making all communication count, that holds true here. Whatever the source of contact—face-to-face, telephone, electronic, written word—creating positive feelings is your job. It's the essence of the relationship."

"It's not simply about all the market analysis I've paid for. It's deeper than that."

"Absolutely, Bill. We're more than statistics and analysis. We're hearts as much as heads. Actually, we're hearts first, and then heads. People make decisions emotionally—Is it relevant? Is it me? Do I trust them?—and then, and only then, do they deal with the rational—features, attributes, pricing."

"I hear you. So once we decide with our heart what we want and where we want to buy and who we want to buy from, then we use our head to punch the numbers."

"And when heart and head meet, at that juncture the purchase is made."

The two men pondered their conversation as Annie slowly walked towards Falcon with Mike and Jessica following right on her heels. All three children had devious grins on their little faces.

"Love you!" She kissed him on the cheek.

"Love you too, Sweet Pea."

"Tag," she tapped his arm. "You're it!"

Laughing, all three children dashed off in different directions, kicking up a cloud of dust behind them. Falcon stood and started jogging after Annie.

"Come on, Bill, help me."

Bill smiled and looked down at his serious wing-tip shoes.

"Oh boy," he said, "another adventure." And with that he ran after Falcon and Annie, her long black hair streaming in back of her, and squeals and shrieks of laughter echoing through the park.

Bill's Notepad

* Perception is truth.

* Our marketing and selling shouldn't be overt. Let our customers get lost in our own brand of magic.

* Subjective reality has its own set of rules. Customers' reality—their truth—is what's important. We can't forget that.

* Make sure to always add to our customers' experience with us.

* Do not follow the Golden Rule. Instead, seek understanding and then give customers what they want. What they uniquely want!

CHAPTER 6

From error to error, one discovers the truth.

~ Sigmund Freud

Bill was undermined, he decided, by his wing-tip shoes. The three children darted behind trees and crawled on their bellies beneath bushes. Falcon wasn't afraid to join them, either. The knees of his overalls were covered in grass stains.

Not in this suit, Bill mused, as he tried to avoid young Jessica's grasp. But, try as he might, and despite the fact that he was once a pretty fair long-distance runner in college, Bill found himself the dreaded "It" for most of the game of tag.

Bill huddled over, trying to catch his breath. Falcon came within three feet of him, as the children fanned out and scattered.

"Now Bill, I realize we've covered a lot of ground today—no pun intended—but I'm only going to stand this close to you. And I'm not going to let you catch me," Falcon smirked playfully.

Bill inhaled deeply, "I don't get it. I used to be able to run circles around anybody."

"Circles Bill, or straight ahead? See, this game is a lot like the market-place today."

"Don't tell me you've found a way to make tag a lesson, Falcon."

"The biggest. Competition is global—no boundaries—and lightening fast. Technology changes at the speed of light. Knowledge is growing exponentially. We suddenly have *too* much information. So what does all that tell you?"

"Not to play tag in serious shoes," Bill joked, looking down at his now-muddied dress shoes.

"True. Dress shoes… they're a metaphor for serious business. But now the corporate culture requires quick reflexes. Athletic shoes, if you will. Look at me," with that, Falcon lifted his foot up. "I got me some 'serious sneakers.' All the better to make me agile, flexible, quick on my feet. And Bill?"

"Yeah?"

"You're still it!" Falcon laughed as he took off across the field with the children.

Bill stopped for a moment. *All this requires is some thought,* he mused. *Who's the weakest runner?* He watched as the children dashed back and forth. He decided that both girls were light on their feet, but Mike was a little slower, and he seemed to get winded more easily. Bill ran off toward Mike.

"Okay, there Buddy, I'm going to catch you," Bill laughed as he drew closer to Mike, who was now laughing and screaming at the same time.

"No way! No way!" Mike shouted over his shoulder. Just as Bill was within inches of him, Mike cut sharply to his right and hopped over a puddle, escaping and catching up to Annie.

"HA! I got away!" Mike yelled out.

Falcon again came within a few feet of Bill.

"Remember the path to success, Bill? That stuff about the customer's truth?"

"Yeah," Bill hunched over, again catching his breath and feeling a twinge in his right knee.

"Well, it changes just like Mike. In an instant and without warning, the customer can be demanding something else entirely—can head off in another direction. And all we can do is try to anticipate and if we don't anticipate the change ahead of time, then we better react. Instantly. Or we'll be in a mud puddle while our competition catches them. And then our competition will have our customer's loyalty, and we'll just be another runner in the pack."

Bill remained hunched over, hands on his knees. "Maybe there's a lesson here. Or maybe I'm just too old for tag."

"Nonsense. You're just thinking too much. Why'd you choose Mike?"

"He stops more often than the girls to catch his breath."

"Nice try. But remember there's a danger in choosing a single direction. Maybe you assumed something that wasn't true. Maybe it was the wrong plan."

"Obviously. I'm over here, and he's way over there. That's my truth."

"Well, as Winston Churchill said, 'Man will occasionally stumble over the truth, but usually manages to pick himself up, walk around it, and carry on.' There's truth here on the field, Bill. You're just ignoring it. In tag, as in business, you have to be willing to get messy."

"Messy?"

"To look for shortcuts. To take chances. Get a few grass stains on the knees. It's just a truth you don't like because of your suit and sensible shoes. The truth is you have to take risks, Bill. Listen… you have a lot of finger-pointing in your company?"

"Doesn't every company? It's not marketing's fault, it's manufacturing's. It's the manager of the sales division. It's the consultant. It's the guy who sells bagels in the morning. It's everyone else's fault."

"But that's not true of every company, is it, Bill?"

"No. Not in companies that are hitting all their numbers."

"That's not true. They still finger-point. And if they don't finger-point, they slap themselves on the back and say 'Me! Me! I did it single-handedly.'"

"Human nature."

"No. I refuse to believe that. I call it a Disease of Inertia."

"Hmm?" Bill stood up and wiped his brow.

"You don't typically see those problems in an entrepreneurial company. Why not?"

"Too busy trying to get started."

"That's just a tiny part of it. No… entrepreneurial companies thrive on innovation; on change. The leader is totally market driven. He or she could care less about seniority, operational status quo, looking foolish… The leader focuses solely on the customer and doing whatever it takes to woo, win, and keep that customer, regardless of whose toes are stepped on or the discomfort it creates."

"Great. But we're not a startup anymore. We've got hundreds of employees and a pretty complex business on our hands."

"I didn't say 'startup'. I said 'entrepreneurial'. Even the best big and complex

EFFECTIVE *leaders don't worry* **about the status quo.**

Business is
MESSY
and always a little
OUT OF
CONTROL.

companies are still entrepreneurial. They all have very detailed plans yet are still flexible. Changing, testing. Testing, measuring. The key is for the leader—you, Bill—to create an environment that rewards innovation. One that embraces failure, instead of simply tolerating it. Let your people see you make mistakes. Make it safe for them to do the same."

"That makes a lot of sense, Falcon. As long as they don't make the same mistake twice. Right?"

"Wrong, Bill. We're talking about a very complex, rapidly changing environment. People are going to make the same mistakes over and over until they become proficient at—and especially comfortable with—the new ways of doing business. If you discourage or punish mistakes, you'll be discouraging experimentation, learning and change. The very disciplines that will keep you in business."

"Hey, you two!" Annie shouted across the field, "Stop talking and start running!"

"Remember, Bill, take risks," Falcon smiled and darted off.

Bill took off after the three kids and Falcon. His feet hurt and his old football knee was reminding him of the time he was tackled while trying to score on a naked bootleg.

"Hey kids! Why don't we play Red Rover? Aren't you tired of tag?"

"No! No!" The three kids shouted back.

"Hey Bill!" Falcon cupped his hands, "Customer innovation demands zigs and zags like tag. You have to make things happen, rather than wait for them to happen. Constantly improve, evolve, grow. Forget about the old 'barriers to entry' game. No one's standing still for Red Rover anymore. Exhausting?"

"Yes!" Bill shouted back.

"If you're going to innovate to achieve customer loyalty, you have to be clever... and quicker."

Bill saw Jessica inching her way toward him as if to tease him a bit. He pretended not to notice her, and then he feigned left, then right, then left again and tried to catch her. Unfortunately, his knee didn't cooperate and he crashed to the ground.

"Bill? You OK?" Falcon trotted over.

"You OK, Mr. West?" Annie asked as the three kids approached the fallen businessman.

"Just a bruised ego."

"Maybe we should stop, kids," Falcon offered.

"Sure, sure, Mr. West. We can stop."

Bill looked up at the four faces now surrounding him. He turned deadly serious and growled, "Not on your life!!" Suddenly he popped up and winked. "No mercy now," he grinned broadly.

The children ran off, but Falcon remained. "You sure you're OK?"

"It dawned on me as I brushed mud off my face, Falcon, I need to play to win. I can't worry about this suit or my serious shoes. Just like if I'm going to turn the company around, I can't worry about playing a flawless game.

PLAY TO
WIN!

Instead, I have to assess constantly. Change rapidly. Make mistakes and move on. Just move, period!"

"George Wald once said, 'We are the products of editing, rather than of authorship.'"

"Well, watch out. Bill West is back in the game!"

Falcon took off downfield, and Bill surveyed the landscape. A large clump of oleander bushes blocked Jessica and Annie from his view. He jogged toward the bushes. The girls were giggling behind them. *They think I'm going to go around,* Bill thought to himself. In a single, perfectly executed movement, he dove beneath the bushes. Branches scratched at him, and he felt mud seeping through the knees of his suit. But he found his target. His left hand grabbed Annie's right sneaker.

"You're 'It,'" he shouted as his head peeked through the branches.

"Yikes!" she squealed and took off after Jessica.

The game progressed for nearly a half-hour as they all ran around the field. Bill could not remember the last time he had sweat or laughed so much.

"Hey kids," Falcon called out, "How about giving a couple of old men a rest? Let's meet at the big oak tree for some story telling."

"YAY!" The kids shouted.

Bill leaned over, sweat dripping from his forehead, breath heaving. "'Play to win,' Falcon says. 'Don't be afraid of getting messy.' My dry cleaner is going to make a killing on my next order," he looked down at his suit.

"OK, so maybe we took the lesson a bit too literally," Falcon smiled, "but business is about trusting your gut. Rules. I love 'em and I hate 'em. I'm not sure there's a rule about not diving under bushes to catch your opponent, but if there is, it was meant to be broken. Beautiful play, by the way."

"Thank you, Coach." Bill ran his hands through his sopping wet hair.

"If you identify your vision in business, Bill, you'll know when to break the rules. You'll say forget the status quo, we're moving forward. Trust your guts, trust your instincts. There's a big difference between following rules and being mindful of values. So go ahead. Create and adapt. Textbooks can inform you, but they can't teach you this stuff. Remember what I said when we first met today? It's all about your experience. Not what I tell you, but what you feel."

"I *feel* wiped out."

"But there's no complacency in tag. You can't flounder mid-field hoping one of the kids will dart by so you can catch 'em."

"That's for sure. Hope had nothing to do with it. This was about surviving."

"Being nimble on your feet."

"Forgetting serious shoes."

"Donning cross-trainers."

"I must have looked like an idiot out there."

"We don't grow by having the answers, Bill. We grow by living the questions. You must be forever searching. And being in sync with our customers—following their lead like following those kids over there—means the occasional mud bath."

Bill suddenly roared with laughter. "Will you look at this shirt? It was white when I left the house this morning."

"You've changed today, Bill."

"I feel that old passion again, Falcon. I sure am changing."

"Change is the key, Bill. Follow the words of Mahatma Gandhi and 'Become the change you want to see in others.'"

The two men arrived at the oak tree where all three kids were lying on their backs, cheeks still flush from the game of tag.

"Story time, kids," Falcon said and got down on the ground with them.

Bill shrugged. "Suit's already ruined," Bill said and settled down on the dirt right next to them.

Bill's Notepad

* Business is messy and always a little out of control.

* Fail. Fail often. But we should fail our way into the future, learning as we go.

* I must embrace failure, not simply tolerate it.

* Play to win!

* Be willing to change directions, to zig and zag as our customers need us to.

* Effective leaders don't worry about the status quo.

* Discovering the truth is an unending journey.

CHAPTER 7

**Give people a fact or an idea and you enlighten their minds;
tell them a story and you touch their souls.**

~ *Hasidic proverb*

Mike, Jessica, and Annie, rosy-cheeked and slightly out of breath gathered in a semi-circle around Falcon and Bill. They were in the shade of a massive oak tree and Annie was gathering acorns in her vicinity and lining them up in front of her.

"You ready kids?" Falcon asked, sitting cross-legged, hands on his knees.

The three children yelled gleefully, "Story time! Story time!"

"OK," Falcon winked at Bill.

Bill smiled, "Finally, a rest from all the lessons."

"What do you mean 'a rest'?" Falcon asked.

"What do you mean, what do I mean? What does telling stories have to do with corporate America? With my slumping sales figures?"

"Bill," Falcon chided, "all this sweating and grass stains, ice cream, and birds, and you haven't picked up on it yet? Lao-Tse wrote it years ago… wise men hear and see as little children do. There's value for you in every experience, if you're aware. But you need to understand that, Bill. When you leave me today, I won't be there to push your thinking into different dimensions. It will be up to you to make connections in your mind where none existed before."

"I understand," said Bill, as Annie and her friends continued stockpiling acorns.

"Do you, Bill? This isn't some kind of pop management theory. It's a way of being. The knowledge you need to succeed will come only from the different perspectives you gain. The perspectives you gain outside your company. Outside your comfort zone."

"Okay. I hear you. I understood about Annie's bird. About the zigging and zagging in tag. But storytelling?"

Falcon turned his attention towards the children and assured them that he'd only be a minute or two more. "Bill, in today's marketplace, which is supersaturated with choice and inundated with information, you need to be known for something. Or to use business jargon—you need a strong brand. It's a necessity. Any guess as to what makes a great brand, Bill?" Falcon raised his eyebrows.

"Alright, Falcon. I'm starting to see these from a mile off. Storytelling?" Bill replied, flashing a broad smile at Falcon.

"Good deduction. See Bill, the great brand is a story. It's not about rattling off features and benefits. It's about meaning and feelings—"

"Because we're all in the feelings business!" Bill chuckled.

"Bill, you are a quick study. Yes… the feelings business. And how do we connect to our customers' and employees' feelings? Through stories. Stories that move them. Stories that connect with their hearts, with their aspirations. Like I said during tag, the pace of change and sweeping technological advances have all but eliminated traditional strategic advantages. You know…. those barriers of entry that you learned about in business school, like economies of scale and control of distribution. Red Rover is over, Bill. A great brand and its growing relationship with customers and employees are really your only remaining strategic advantages. Get it?"

"Got it!"

"Good. Now let's tell these kids some stories before they steal every squirrel's acorn under this tree!"

Falcon turned to the three children who now settled down from their acorn hoarding and were wide-eyed with anticipation. "So who has a story to share with me and Bill today?"

Mike started waving his hand wildly in the air. Falcon playfully pretended he didn't see Mike's excitement.

"What? No one has a story today? I can't believe it! You kids always have stories. But I guess this is going to be one of those days—"

Mike could stand it no longer, "I do! I do, Mr. Falcon!"

"Oh. Mike? Mike has a story. I didn't even see his hand up there."

The children all giggled. "Story please," Annie said, as this was clearly a ritual the children enjoyed.

"Well… today I was wicked nervous when I left for school. Today… was …" Mike whispered, "…report card day."

"And?" said Bill.

"And last night I dreamed three monsters came to get me. Not just any monsters. Huge scary looking monsters with big fangs and green teeth. And big glow-in-the-dark red eyes. And this morning, I peeked under my bed for those monsters, but they weren't there. So I knew they were waiting for me at school. I thought I saw them behind every tree. And in the cafeteria. The monsters were everywhere until I got my report card. And then… when I opened my report card—"

"Yes?" said Jessica expectantly.

"They disappeared. Poof." Mike gazed skyward and made a flourish with his hands. "Because… I got three A's and two B's."

Falcon slapped his knee. "That's the best news, Mike. The best! You should be very proud of yourself. That's quite a leap from last year."

Mike nodded, grinning broadly. "I've got brains in every corner of my head."

"You sure do, Mike. Congratulations." Bill said, as the two little girls each gave Mike a high-five.

When everyone had settled down, Falcon spoke. "So tell me, Mike, what do you think made the difference this year?"

"You know how you're always telling us to believe in ourselves, Mr. Falcon?" Falcon nodded.

"Well, this year it's a lot easier to do that. I like myself a lot better with my new teacher."

"Your new teacher?" asked Bill.

Falcon interjected, "Sure. A teacher is the CEO of the classroom. He or she has the power to make the children believe they can do it. Believe it's right there—within their grasp. The magic monster potion."

"I could use some of that monster potion myself."

"That magic monster potion is yours to have Bill. Simply combine mutual respect with a lot of open communication, and a healthy dose of supportive leadership. I call it spirit enhancement. Don't squash a child's spirit—or a child-like spirit—nurture it."

"Isn't this getting a little touchy-feely?"

"Not at all. We're in the—"

Bill laughed in spite of himself, "The feelings business. OK. I think I got that one."

"Do you Bill? Feelings… what's another word we can use? We keep coming back to this point. Maybe feelings make us—in the business world—a little uncomfortable. How about passion? You see Bill, only the passions—and the passionate—have the ability to inspire, to persuade. And when you're passionate, how do you communicate with others? You tell a story. A personal anecdote. You wave your arms about like Mike there."

"From the heart."

"Always from the heart. You try. Tell the kids a story."

"I'm not very good at this sort of thing."

"Sure you are. It's a lot easier than you think."

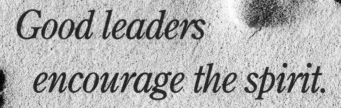

Good leaders encourage the spirit.

It's about feelings. **Stories create** *intimacy* **and** *relationships.*

"PLEEEEASE!!!!!!" A chorus of voices urged him on.

Bill sighed. *First tag, now fairy tales. I'm not sure about this.* "OK. Here goes." He looked at the upturned faces, then down at the ground. And suddenly, a story from his childhood flew into his mind.

"Hand me that acorn, Annie." She complied and handed him the smallest acorn on her pile.

"See this acorn?"

The children nodded.

"This acorn's name is Arnie. And Arnie is the smallest acorn in the park. In fact, he is so small that he might be the smallest acorn on record anywhere. We're talking Guinness Book of World Records small. But Arnie's parents always told him, 'Arnie, have no fear because deep within you is the potential to be the biggest oak in the forest. A giant among trees.'"

"Of course, Arnie heard this, but he didn't really believe it because a lot of the other acorns made fun of him. They told him he was too scrawny to ever amount to anything. But Arnie's father, the mightiest oak in the park, told him not to worry. And after a while, Arnie stopped listening to the other acorns. Instead, he listened to the still, small acorn voice inside of himself that told him 'You can become a giant oak, Arnie, if only you believe.'"

Bill found himself drawn into his own story. He was changing his voice to the character of Arnie.

"And so, one spring, after a long, cold, snowy winter, Arnie set down his roots. He told himself, 'Believe, Arnie. Believe.' By now, the other acorn voices were a distant echo. And sure enough, he felt himself growing tall." Bill stood and stretched his hands towards the clouds.

"With each passing year, his roots grew deeper into the earth, and he felt connected to every living thing. Soon, he was nudging above all the other trees until finally… finally… he was the tallest in the park. By then, he was very wise, and often little acorns came to him for advice and wisdom. And always, always, Arnie took the time to tell them his own life story. 'You can be mighty,' he told them. 'You can become a giant, if only you believe.' And Arnie lived happily ever after."

The children clapped and cheered their approval. "That was the *best* story," said Jessica, as Annie and Mike nodded their approval.

Bill glanced at Falcon, suddenly self-conscious. He shrugged, "It was the best I could do on short notice."

"That was great! You see Bill, the best stories aren't necessarily long-winded or once-upon-a-time tales. And they don't have to be humorous with some big punch line. Storytelling is really just a way to express your message so that it comes alive. Ones that excite the imagination and engage the listener. And I think you did that very well. Our friends here were plenty engaged. They'll never forget little Arnie… or you, Bill."

"Thanks, Falcon."

"And Bill?"

"Ya, Falcon." Falcon reached over and grabbed him tightly around the shoulder.

"Don't forget," he added, grinning broadly, "an oak was just a nut that stood its ground."

Just then, Mike and Jessica jumped to their feet and waved towards the parking lot. "That's our sitter," said Jessica. "We got to go. Bye everyone."

"Bye Jessica," said Bill and Falcon, as Jessica hugged Annie and ran off across the field.

"Bye Mr. West. Oh, and look…" Mike held up an acorn.

"What's that?"

"Arnie. A good luck charm."

Bill winked at Mike. Just remember… believe, Mike."

Mike smiled and nodded, and broke out into a full sprint to catch up with Jessica.

After they were down the hill and out of sight, Bill turned to Annie and Falcon.

"What great kids." Falcon nodded and winked at his granddaughter.

"They sure are. And great soccer players, too. Right Annie?"

"Right, coach," Annie smiled.

Bill grinned and shook his head, "You coach, too? You are full of surprises and energy, Falcon. So, you two hungry?"

Both nodded. "OK. My treat. Anywhere you want. What do you like to eat?"

"HAMBURGERS!" They both said, in perfect unison.

Annie laughed, "Personal jinx! Pinch, poke," she pinched and poked her grandfather, "you owe me a Coke. You're wearing black. You owe me a pack."

Falcon smiled ruefully, "I never remember to do that jinx thing. She beats me to the punch every single time!"

"Well… today that Coke's on me, too. Come on, you two. Let's go eat—somewhere where grass stains won't cause a scene."

The two men each took Annie by the hand and the three of them headed away from Arnie the acorn and the great oak tree and into the fading sun. Bill turned back and stared at the oak and the fields where he'd acquired his grass and mud stains. He stuck his free hand into his pants pocket. He'd absentmindedly put an acorn there. *This is more than just an afternoon of fun and games, Bill, he said to himself. Like the acorn, you just need to believe.*

Bill's Notepad

* Red Rover is over.

* Magic monster potion is created only by adding leadership that does not crush the child-like spirit.

* We must be consistent in all our stories; our stories must match our behavior.

* Kids communicate with no inhibitions. They speak from the heart. Strive to communicate person-to-person, heart-to-heart in everything we do.

* Stories create intimacy and relationships. And that's the essence of a strong brand.

* Have everyone share stories and listen to stories. Especially stories from our customers.

CHAPTER 8

To know even one life has breathed easier because you have lived, this is to have succeeded.

~ Ralph Waldo Emerson

They arrived at Falcon's and Annie's favorite hamburger restaurant named The King's. Elvis Presley glossy photos and memorabilia hung on every available inch of wall space. Elvis dolls and swivel-hipped singing knickknacks adorned shelves. And of course, Elvis crooned out over the restaurant's sound system.

After following Falcon's recommendation and ordering two burgers with "the works," and a cheeseburger and chocolate shake for Annie, Bill leaned back against his side of the booth.

"You know Annie, your Grandpa's a pretty terrific guy, to watch your two soccer buddies on Thursdays, and to coach your team. I'm going to have to come to a game, now, you know." Annie smiled.

"That would be GREAT, Mr. West."

"Blue Suede Shoes" came on over the sound system as the waitress brought their drinks and a children's activity paper with crayons for Annie.

"Thank you, Ma'am," Annie smiled.

"Your welcome, young lady," the waitress smiled back.

"What have you got there, Annie?" Bill asked as Annie took her green crayon and began working on the puzzles and games on the paper.

"This puzzle." She showed Bill the classic nine-dot puzzle. "I have to use only four straight lines, and I can't lift up my crayon. And I have to connect *all* these dots."

"That's a tough one."

Annie nodded and bent her head in concentration.

"You know Bill, I've seen a consultant use this puzzle in a workshop. He talked about *mental* boxes and needing to think *outside* the box."

"Yeah. I've heard that before with a different prop."

"But you know, I don't think it's really about mental boxes."

"It isn't?" Bill looked puzzled.

"It's about physical boxes—our homes and our businesses. We go back and forth, back and forth, like rats in mazes. And sure, maybe we brainstorm here and there and try to think outside the box. Maybe we hire the best creative staff money can buy."

"Sounds familiar," Bill said, ruefully.

"Sure. You can come up with limitless ideas, but if you don't break out of your routine, if you don't connect to the bigger reality outside your physical box, all the creative ideas in the world won't help you. And what do you think is the most important puzzle to master?"

"Breaking routine?"

"To do what?" Falcon leaned forward. "Take it another level higher."

Bill shrugged. "Enlighten me, Falcon."

"The most important puzzle to master is understanding and communicating with your audience. Figuring out what people want and giving it to them. Helping them get the positive feelings they want, and eliminating the negative ones which they *don't* want."

"Falcon, again, it seems so *obvious.* I don't know…"

"But it isn't so obvious. What people think about you or your company is unimportant, Bill. What matters is how you make them feel about *themselves* and *their* decisions in your presence." Have you heard the story about Benjamin Disraeli?"

"Nineteenth-century British Prime Minister?"

Falcon nodded. "Yes. The story I'm thinking of is about a young woman who dined one night with William Gladstone—another eminent statesman at the time. The next night, Disraeli accompanied her to dinner. And the woman later said, 'When I left the dining room after sitting next to Mr. Gladstone, I thought he was the most clever man in all of England. But after sitting next to Mr. Disraeli, I was sure that I was the most clever woman in England.'"

"Apparently she had a memorable encounter with Mr. Disraeli."

"Sure. The feelings he stirred in her about *herself* lingered long after the dinner was over. And that's your job, Bill, and the job of everyone in your organization. You have to enhance your customers' experiences with you each and every time they see you. And by you, I mean your people, your ads, your packaging, everything. That's the secret of capturing loyalty."

Annie looked up from her puzzle. "I did it!"

Both men looked at the paper and her green crayon marks.

"Good job, Annie," Falcon said. "You used your thinking cap. That's not an easy puzzle.

"Thank you, Grandpa." Annie beamed.

"Your Grandpa sure believes in you, Annie."

"Mm-hmm. He helped me learn this puzzle. And he tells me every day something good to believe about me. And now… it's gotten so I tell myself something good. That way, if anyone picks on me or says something not nice at school, then I just remember the good stuff and I don't feel so sad inside."

Bill looked at the two of them. "My guru and my teacher. You know, I'm starting to put this all together. If I can get each of my people to feel believed in and supported, then we can do anything as a company. It isn't about formulas. It's about heart-to-heart."

Falcon smiled. "A lesson well-learned, Bill."

Their dinners arrived and Bill felt himself overcome by hunger. "I sure worked up an appetite playing tag, Annie."

"Me, too!" She exclaimed as she grabbed a French fry and smothered it in ketchup.

"So Falcon, when I leave you two tonight and I go back to the office, can it really be this simple? I mean, the marketplace is different from when you were at the top of your game. Advertising clutter, e-mail, media fragmentation… How do I get my customers to listen to us . . . to our brand? How does my company become, pardon the pun, 'The King'?"

"The marketplace is different?" Falcon asked.

"Sure," said Bill, biting into his burger.

"Wait just a minute." Falcon fumbled in his coveralls for a small black

People need to

feel believed in

and *feel* supported,

then they can do anything.

book. "I keep some of my favorite quotes in here. Are you ready?"

Bill nodded and Falcon read from the page he turned to. "Psychologists tell us the mind is under a continual bombardment of ideas, all of which are trying to make an impression upon it. The activities of a man's business that are going on about him, the people around him, the ideas that he has in mind to work out, the train of thought started by some object on which his vision rests—to say nothing of such commonplace things as his morning mail, his telephone and the papers on his desk—all claim his attention. And what is more, there is insistent demand that he attend immediately to one or several of these things. The prospect, therefore, does not sit around with his mind a blank, calmly waiting for someone or something to capture his attention without a struggle. The salesman enters a field already well occupied and must fight for the undivided attention that is essential to a successful sale. He must, by his personality, his proposition and by his opening remarks, eliminate all competitors for that attention and hold the field alone."

"You got it, Falcon. Exactly. I'm not telling you something you didn't already know."

Falcon laughed. "That's right. The book this quote is from—*Modern Business*—was published in 1918. You see, Bill, getting someone's attention has *always* been a challenge… and *always* will be."

"1918, huh? Okay then, how *do* you get their attention?"

"Well first let me tell you how *not* to do it. Forget about being loud or outrageous to be heard. Because only communication that connects will be listened to. Also, don't we all believe that the more we say, the more people will pay attention to us. It's simply not true. Rather, it's about relevance. Haven't you ever been at a party, involved in conversation, when all of a sudden you hear your name come up in another conversation? You were *hearing* the other conversation all along, but it wasn't until you heard your name—something that really matters to you—that you became aware of the other conversation."

"No handstands," Annie piped in.

"I beg your pardon?" Bill asked.

"No handstands, no grandstands. Grandpa likes people who don't tell you that they're important. Everyone's important. Like Mr. Crenshaw."

"Mr. Crenshaw?"

"Dan Crenshaw is a fine old gentleman. And he has a Studebaker that's his pride and joy. But he doesn't have a lot of money for repairs. And when he comes in, I make sure we take good care of his old car—just as much as we care for Bradley Hopper's cars."

"You take care of Brad Hopper's cars?"

"All thirty-seven of them. But I sometimes find the fact that he reminds me—every time he comes in—that he owns this and that and runs such and such businesses a little tiresome. That's not a story. That's a handstand."

As the trio finished their burgers, Bill pondered his leadership. Did everyone he come in contact with feel important? Did he make each and every contact count? Could the answer not be in the spreadsheets and instead be in humility and empathy?

When they had finished, Bill grabbed the bill. "It's on me, don't forget."

"Time to get this little Missy home to bed," Falcon said as he slid out of the booth. "Mind if we stop by my garage first?"

"Not at all."

The three of them stood to leave. Bill looked down at Annie's table mat.

"Can I have this, Annie? I like your doodles. And the way you solved your puzzle. I'd like to hang this on my wall at work."

Annie grinned. "Sure. I'll even draw you a picture of my dog Honey to give to you next time. I draw her really good 'cause I see her all the time, and I know every little thing about her."

Bill winked. "I'd like that." He picked up the table mat. *Live outside the box. Break your routine. Connect the dots with empathy and compassion. The green crayon of an innocent child. A child not yet defined by rules, routines and narrow thinking.* Bill West smiled broadly. He could solve the puzzle now.

Bill's Notepad

* We must all live, as well as think outside the box if the company is going to succeed.

* It doesn't matter what people think about us. What matters is how we make them feel about themselves and their decisions in our presence.

* Connect the dots with compassion and empathy.

* Just as children respond to praise, so will my people.

* Gaining trust from the marketplace is more about connections than who can draw the most attention to themselves.

CHAPTER 9

**The highest reward that God gives us for good work
is the ability to do better work.**

~ Elbert Hubbard

On the ride to the station, Annie pulled a stuffed animal from her backpack and curled up with it in the back seat. Before they were on the road five minutes, she was sound asleep.

Bill turned around and looked at the sleeping child. In the pale light of the moon and highway lights, Annie's long lashes cast shadows on her cheeks. Her face was absolutely serene, like a photograph.

"You're a lucky guy, Falcon. She's beautiful, and she's certainly full of… I don't know… a love of people. The world hasn't battered her around yet. She has such enthusiasm."

"You know, we adults tend to feel the world is falling apart. And we want more intimacy because there's so much change in the world. So much we can't control. It just seems that children know how to grasp connections instantly. They have no artifice, and they aren't interested in holding you at arm's length."

"You know, Falcon, today seemed like such a long day to me. Not long in a bad way. It's just that when I'm at work, the day flies by, and all of a sudden I'm looking at my watch and it's 5:30. Today, it felt like it went in slow motion. We did so many different things, had fun with the kids… talked."

"I know what you mean."

"You want to know the scary thing?" Bill asked.

"What?"

"I feel like my life has flown by the last twenty years. Where did it go?

The time? You know, when I was in college, I would have called a guy my age 'old.'"

"If you're old then I'm ancient," Falcon laughed.

"Today just… I don't know… opened my mind about a few things."

"Bill, you want to know why life seems to pass so much slower when we're with kids… when we're being kids?"

"Yeah. Enlighten me. It was truly a strange feeling today."

"Okay. Well, when we're with children, and when we think like children—when we were children—every experience was fresh and new and exciting. So, you want your life to slow down? Then experience each day as the new.

Soon, the three of them were pulling into the parking lot of Falcon's garage. Falcon gathered Annie up into his arms, being careful not to wake her, and carried her inside where he placed her gently on a large sofa in his office. He then covered little Annie with a large comforter and kissed her on the cheek.

Falcon turned towards Bill and whispered. "Want to see two of my other beauties?"

"Sure," Bill shrugged.

Falcon walked over to a garage in the back. When he turned on the lights, Bill remarked, "This is a garage? It's so clean you could eat off the floor."

"Passion breeds care."

Falcon moved over to two cars and flicked on a second light so Bill could

You *get out* of your *relationships,*
what you *put into* them.

get a good look. Bill let out a long, slow whistle. "Wow!"

"Yup. This one's a '56 Chevy Belair Convertible."

"The two-tone red and white paint job is fantastic. What a car!" Bill said as he walked around the car, admiring the paint and the chrome.

"Now this one here," Falcon moved over to the second car, a shiny white one, "is a 1953 Corvette. Only 300 were produced, and 200 were known to

Experience each day
as *new* and *fresh.*

have survived. This baby is a real gem. I've been restoring her for longer than any other car I've worked on. The parts are nearly impossible to find."

"You're right. A beauty if I ever saw one. She's perfect."

Falcon moved around to the car's right front side. "Perfect. Except she's missing one hubcap here. Been looking everywhere for one. Calling in all my favors. No hubcap."

"Well, she's magnificent just the same."

"Thanks."

Falcon turned off the lights as the two men left the garage.

"I got a lot out of my day today, Falcon. I wasn't too sure when we started … that seems like it was days ago. But now…"

"Relationships are like mirrors, Bill. You get out of them what you put into them."

"Well, I had a great one today, Falcon. You opened my eyes."

"All the answers to your problems were in your head all along, Bill. You just needed to tap into your heart to unlock them. Leadership is all about giving, not receiving."

"I can't thank you enough. And I would like to go to one of Annie's soccer games. Mind if I call you to set it up?"

"Bill, we're friends now. Call anytime."

They shook hands, and Falcon slapped Bill on the back. Bill climbed into his car and waved good-bye as he drove away.

Bill West mulled over the day again and again, smiling at key points as he reflected on the lessons he learned. He drove across town to his home and pulled into his driveway. He knew his wife would be at her weekly book group, so the house was dark, and he fumbled for his keys at the door.

Entering his house, his menagerie of pets greeted him and he fed, walked and watered the cat and his dogs. He fed the fish and his birds; it was always his way to unwind after a busy day. Then he went upstairs to take off his grass-stained clothes and to shower.

In his bedroom, he picked up his portable phone as he flicked on the light. It was habit. He dialed his voice mail.

The electronic voice spoke, "You have… 15 new messages."

He sighed, and started listening to them.

"Bill, this is Ray. Croton and Sons reneged on the deal. We need to talk about a counter-offer. This is a colossal pain. I don't need to tell you how many hours I put into this…" Beep.

"Bill? Karen. Listen, I need to know what you want me to do about the Morris account. He insists if we don't do better on price this year he is going to drop us. But we've kept him at the same price for three years now. I vote for letting him go. Where else is he going to get a deal like ours?" Beep.

Bill West felt himself fall naturally into "CEO"-mode. He pressed 8 on his phone to respond to Karen, his back muscles tightening.

"Karen, Bill here. Listen, I think we need to have a sit-down with Morris.

I don't like that he keeps holding our feet to the fire. Talk to me first thing tomorrow. Friday."

He listened to the next voice mail. "Bill. Randy Black here. Listen, I get the impression that your sales manager thinks he can screw around with what has been a long-standing agreement between us. This is a bunch of nonsense and you know it." Beep.

"Bill, this is Marv…"

Bill continued listening to his voice mail, growing tenser by the moment, as he walked over to his dresser. He kept an old cigar box on his dresser that belonged to his grandfather. He opened it with one hand as he started emptying his change and receipts into the box. Quarters, nickels, and dimes clinked against the existing change. He was still listening intently to his messages when an acorn landed on the change.

"Arnie," he whispered. Suddenly, the voice mail seemed a thousand miles away. He clicked off the phone and placed it on his dresser. A rush of shock filled him. How could he have forgotten everything so quickly, slipped back into the old mind-set? The old way of doing things? He picked up the acorn and stared at it.

"If we're going to be mighty, I need to live each day like today… at the park. Playing tag." He was aware he was whispering to himself. "The genius of childhood, Arnie, my friend. The genius of childhood."

Shaken by how tense he had allowed himself to get, Bill went over to his bed and sat down. The day seemed very long as he sat there reflecting on his life when he heard his wife come into the house.

"Bill?" she called.

"Up here, Honey."

He sat on the bed, waiting for her to make her way up the stairs.

"You're just getting home?" she asked, noting he was still half-dressed in his suit.

"Yeah, Hon. Sit down. I've had the most amazing day."

She sat beside him, and he grasped her hand.

"I have so much to tell you," he said softly, as he began. "It all started when I met this guy Falcon at a gas station…"

Bill's Notepad

* Experience each day as new and fresh.

* We crave intimacy in this fast-paced world where everything seems out of control.

* I'll get out of my relationships, what I put into them.

* I must give, not receive, if I expect to be a great leader.

* The answers are all inside of me.

CHAPTER *10*

There go my people. I must follow them,
for I am their leader.

~ *Gandhi*

Falcon steered his white Corvette through the summer sun, the brilliant sheen of the well-polished car bouncing the rays of the sun off its hood and literally gleaming. He didn't drive the Corvette often, but today was a special day. The car was perfect, except for the missing hubcap; she was the best restoration he had ever done.

Glancing to his right, Falcon saw that Annie was engrossed in a book. "What are you reading, Annie?"

"A biography of Helen Keller, Grandpa."

"But it's summer," he teased. "Why are you reading books?"

"Books are the key to knowledge, Grandpa. Books and experience. You know that."

"Do I?"

Annie laughed, her smile revealing two newly grown front teeth. "Yes! You're the one who told me that. Stop being so silly."

Falcon grinned. Annie always said what was on her mind. He looked up at a highway sign. According to the directions, he had four more exits to go. As he drove, he noticed people speeding up to catch a closer glimpse of the Corvette, and he smiled to himself. Finally, he reached their exit and made a right-hand turn. On the corner was the church Bill told him about. The pastor was nearly as fond as Falcon of sayings, and he displayed them on a sign in the church's front yard. "Faith is caught, not taught."

"Ain't that the truth," Falcon whispered to himself.

He drove down a short stretch of road and into an industrial park. He found the building.

"Come on, Annie," he said as he parked the car and helped his granddaughter scramble out.

Walking through the front entrance of Bill's company, Falcon sensed an electricity in the air. The first thing he noticed was the activity. As employees walked through the lobby on their way to meetings or other parts of the building, they walked in clusters, clearly engrossed in their conversations. Falcon also noticed something else. Smiling. Joking. He overheard one exchange in which the two people disagreed with each other, but they each listened and fully acknowledged the other. The conversations were both playful and provocative, friendly, yet they were clearly unafraid to speak their minds. Falcon nodded his head in silent approval.

"Good morning, Sir!" An older man stopped and smiled at Falcon and kneeled down to shake Annie's hand, "how can I help you two?"

Falcon spoke, "I'm Richard Falcon, and this here is my granddaughter, Annie."

"This is Miss Annie Bananie?"

Annie giggled and nodded. The man lifted her up and gave her a little spin, placing her back down again.

"Well, I'll be… and Falcon. *The* Falcon. Let me shake your hand. I'm John Stasinos. And it is truly a pleasure to meet you. Bill told us you were coming. You know, after he met with you, he came back and told us a story. In fact, he told us many stories, but he told us one important one about a day he spent with you and Annie here and…" John hesitated for a moment.

"Go on," Falcon smiled.

"Well, he told us that we weren't employees anymore. We were all part of the solution. He said he would never give up and he wouldn't let us fail."

"Sounds like a powerful meeting."

"It was," John looked Falcon in the eyes. "A few people were wiping their eyes. Bill was very emotional too. Before that meeting with you, we all thought maybe we'd be looking for new jobs soon. But after that…" John shook his head, the memory clearly a strong one. "Well, put it this way, I feel like six months ago I did get a new job at a new company—only I never left this one. And look at the wall over there."

"The spot where the paint's a different color?" Annie asked.

"Yeah. That's where we used to have a sign. A mission statement. Only it really didn't mean much to us. To any of us. It was just a fancy-sounding paragraph. So Bill took it down. But he asked us not to repaint over the spot, made us keep it looking different. So that when we came in every day, we would remember… how did he put it? That we are more than a mission statement. We are living a mission." John Stasinos paused. "Oh look." He smiled broadly and gestured with his hand as if he were introducing a celebrity. "Here he comes."

Falcon and Annie turned and Annie darted off in a spontaneous run. Bill lifted her up and gave her a big bear hug, carrying her back to Falcon and John.

"Is your hair faintly pink, Bill?" Falcon laughed as the two men shook hands.

"Lost a bet with my marketing department. This is very faded. You should have seen it Wednesday."

"I can attest," John was laughing out loud. "He looked like a refugee from a punk rock band."

"Annie?"

"Yes, Mr. West?"

"Do you want to go with John here? Today is Freaky Friday in the lunchroom. All the employees bring their kids to eat with them, and we have entertainment. I think today is a magician. And we have a special menu in the cafeteria, including a table where you can make your own ice cream sundae. I bet, because I knew you were coming, there's even some peppermint stick."

"You remembered!"

"Would never forget, Annie."

"Can I go, Grandpa?"

"Sure, Sweetie. See you later."

John took her by the hand and led her off.

"I didn't know what to expect Bill. But I sense it. The place is alive."

"Thanks Falcon. It certainly hasn't been easy."

"Helping people change the way they think never is, Bill."

"Well, I started thinking, I had all these smart people. Great people with great ideas. But we needed some balance. We needed the feelings side. We

WORK should be *fun!*

BELIEVE IT!
and uncover the intuition.

lost it—or maybe we never had it. Anyway, care for the nickel tour?"

The two men went from department to department. Everywhere Falcon was impressed by the palpable excitement in the air.

"When I came back from our meeting, I thought a lot about branding," Bill whispered so as not to disturb the team. "So I gathered this team together, and we talked about the feelings business."

"I wonder where you ever got that crazy idea," Falcon winked.

"Have no idea," Bill playfully replied. "But we talked about feelings nonetheless. And everyone kept coming back to design. From advertising to Web site design to product design… we decided no more functionality without beauty. Aesthetics are important. It equals feelings. So we made a connection between our designs and excited, happy customers."

"And a brand was born."

"You got it."

"This team here takes their work very seriously, but not themselves. Work should be fun. Can you believe I'm saying that? Can you believe I know that… I believe it with all my soul. My people, their sense of fun, this branding… we're achieving results we've never experienced before. Out of sight."

"That's the essence of uncovering the intuitive."

"Right," Bill motioned Falcon down a hallway. "My people sense this intuitively. They're moving toward the realm of unconscious competency."

"Now that's a new one to me."

"See, there's unconscious incompetence. You don't even know what you don't know."

"OK. I got you," Falcon nodded.

"Then there's conscious incompetence. You're aware of what you don't know. And there's conscious competence. You know what you know."

"Like I know you look ridiculous with pink hair?"

Bill gave Falcon a sidelong glance. "Yeah, wiseguy. Sort of like that. And then there's unconscious competence. Like artists. You don't even know what you know. You can just do it. It's part of you."

"I hear you. I'm going to remember that one."

The two men walked down another hall toward the cafeteria.

"This has been the hardest six months of my life. But the most rewarding. My employees are my friends… my family. I feel excited again. Passionate… the way your granddaughter is. And watching them—us—grow and learn and excel… it's a joy."

"Isn't it though? You've got real teamwork and innovation going on here. People not afraid to approach you, not afraid to make mistakes."

"Like my hair. Not afraid to get muddy… or look foolish. It's about giving up the compulsion to control everything. Freedom from the grind. The e-mails I can let go of. The voice mails someone else can handle. The nonessential stuff can wait. The people and feelings can't."

The two men entered the cafeteria where it appeared most of the company had gathered. Annie ran over to Falcon.

117

The nonessential
stuff can wait.

The *people* and *feelings*

CAN'T WAIT.

"Grandpa… they have a cake! For us. For me and you!!"

She led him by the hand to a table where a cake sat. It was white, and on the top was an elaborate icing picture. It was a sandbox with a red bucket in it. Across the top of the sheet cake were the words, "Sandbox wisdom will release your inner child." Across the bottom of the cake was "To Annie and Falcon with love!!"

Falcon was deeply touched. He squeezed Annie's hand and pulled her close to him. She had the wisdom. He had merely learned to absorb it instead of being caught up, as Bill had once been, in all of the day-to-day minutiae.

"Everyone," Bill shouted, as he climbed atop a chair, "I want to gather you all together. Come on over here."

The employees gathered around the cake table. Excitement rippled through the crowd.

"As you all know, we owe a debt of gratitude to Falcon and Annie here. I personally do, and you all know how we've all changed thanks to the lessons and insights I learned from them. I know Falcon. He wouldn't like the words 'debt of gratitude.'"

Falcon nodded in agreement.

"So I merely want to say, 'Thank you friends.' And I would like you to have these gifts."

Bill handed Annie a wrapped present. She quickly tore it open. "A book!"

"Arnie the Acorn," Falcon whispered and ran his finger across the title. "Marcy West?"

"My wife. She always wanted to write a book and illustrate it. I just encouraged her to follow her dream. We self-published it. Can't keep enough in print."

"Thank you," Annie clutched the book to her chest.

"And Falcon…" Bill handed him a package. Falcon tore open the paper, as all the employees leaned forward in anticipation. Inside the box was a shiny hubcap.

"Oh my… " Falcon felt himself choke up. He looked up, "How did you…?"

"I didn't do anything."

A chorus of voices in the room said, "We did!"

Bill explained. "I couldn't find it Falcon, so I turned it over to the most dedicated team I know. All of them. They found it. I am totally convinced. They can do anything. Plus. . ." Bill added with a smile. "No one is as smart as everyone."

"Thank you," Falcon said genuinely moved. "I'm grateful I could be some small part of this energy."

"Come on," Bill said, "Let's cut this cake."

After cake and coffee, it was time for Falcon and Annie to go. Bill walked them to the front door.

"Stay true to your wisdom, Bill."

"I will, Falcon."

He bent down to hug Annie. "And you… you stay true to all you feel inside, Annie."

"I will, Mr. West." She kissed his cheek.

Annie and Falcon left the building and walked to the Corvette. Falcon opened his trunk and pulled out a tool, placing the hubcap on the bare wheel. He stood up and stepped back.

"What do you think, Annie?"

"It's beautiful!"

Falcon tousled her hair. "Let me get you home."

The two of them drove away. Falcon looked in his rearview mirror. "Look behind us Annie."

She turned around. A couple of dozen employees were waving as they left the parking lot. Annie waved furiously until they were out of sight. Soon, they were on the open highway, the Corvette gleaming in the setting sun.

"Grandpa?"

"Yeah, Love bug?"

"That day? That day with the sandbox and the bird, and the ice cream and all?"

"Yeah…"

"Did it really help Mr. West that much? I mean, he gave me this book and everything."

"Yes, Sweetie. But here's a secret. All those changes he made to his company? They were inside him all the time. He just sort of forgot. See, grownups get big and they forget all the things they know about people and love and feelings. It just gets lost in all the seriousness of being a grown-up."

"Do grownups have to be so serious?"

"No, Sweetie, they don't. Not at all."

"Does everybody have those things inside them?"

"Yes, Annie they do. They just forget. Luckily, I have you, so I can't ever forget."

Richard Falcon drove down the highway toward the setting sun. He glanced over at Annie. He had his hubcap. He had feelings in his life. He had sandbox wisdom and, most importantly, he would never let it go.

Bill's Notepad

* It's all about FAITH...
  and love.

Tom Asacker

Tom Asacker is often described as a catalyst and a nonconformist. He is an independent brand strategy advisor and an internationally acclaimed speaker. He is also the author of *A Little Less Conversation: Connecting with Customers in a Noisy World* and *A Clear Eye for Branding: Straight Talk on Today's Most Powerful Business Concept.*

Beyond his success as an author and speaker, Tom is a former corporate executive and an accomplished entrepreneur. He is a recipient of the George design awards; and is recognized by Inc. Magazine, MIT, and the Young Entrepreneurs' Organization as a past member of their Birthing of Giants entrepreneurial executive leadership program.

Today, Tom helps professionals and organizations transition from being economically-driven to feelings-driven, and thus grow their brands by connecting deeply with their audiences. You can find out more about Tom and his philosophies by visiting www.acleareye.com.